CONSIEOSOPHY
By: Prince Nasir Akim Bey

Published by Majestic
Publishing Group Inc.
Copyright 2018

CONSIEOSOPHY

CONSIEOSOPHY:

Knowledge through observation.

Understanding life through experience.

DEDICATION

This book is dedicated to the seeker

SPECIAL THANKS

To Ms. Rosemary Lopez for her many years of support and belief in my work.

INTRODUCTION

Consieosophy is a field of learning that allows the thinking mind to review the world and all of its properties from a realistic, tangible, and coherent perspective, as opposed to a proposed one. The minds of the human race have been so severely compromised by belief systems, propaganda, and occult popularities, that it has become virtually impossible for man kind to accurately comprehend itself without the involvement of these systems being an intrinsic part of the process. Man has not been given the spiritual and mental information needed to accurately secure his existence on this planet without injuring himself or others. Therefore, he finds himself lost within a whirlwind of rhetoric, motivational jargon, and inspirational malarkey that has no real effect on the ethereal mind but has a great effect on the corporate mind and its regulations. A mind that has been systematically programmed cannot deactivate other programs but only regulate them. Therefore, what appears to be helpful information that will infuse a growth spurt within the thinking mind, is only a regulatory tool used to keep the mind occupied on things that play no real part in the evolution of the living being. Now, in order to find solutions to the problems we encounter when it comes to the human mind and his thinking patterns, we have to first discover the anatomy of the mind and its true functionality. The first question we all must ask ourselves is: what is the mind? To answer questions like what constitutes the mind and what properties make up the mind, one must organically apply the critical thinking skills that would allow him to discover the truth about his inherent makeup. Since the only truth we know of in reference to who we are is a truth that was given to us and not discovered by us, it always makes humanity susceptible to mistakes and irreversible consequences. Consieosophy allows the thinking mind to discover the truth without prejudice and influence. The consieosophist is someone who is always in search of broadening his knowledge about life, himself, and the human soul.

LESSON PLAN

LESSON 1: *THE ETHEREAL BEING*

LESSON 2: *ANATOMY*

LESSON 3: *INTELLIGENCE*

LESSON 4: *CONSCIOUSNESS*

LESSON 5: *ALCHEMY*

QUOTABLE QUOTES

LESSON 1: THE ETHEREAL BEING

Life on this planet that we call Earth is regarded to be a mystery by the human race. But it is only a mystery because the interest in finding out the real reason why Earth and its inhabitants exist has been substituted by the enjoyment of the properties that make up life itself. Consieosophy is the knowledge, study, and anatomy of the ethereal being that animates energy through every property of life. It is the knowledge of what life truly is in contrast to what has been proposed to us, and is the process of acquiring knowledge through observation and understanding the world through experience. Now, the ethereal being that this branch of philosophy refers to is the being that lives in every living thing that roams the face of this planet. To better understand the "being," we must first grasp an accurate understanding of what it actually is. A being is an existence and a presence that cannot be seen by the physical eye but can only be seen through various illustrations of life.

This presence is not only experiencing life through its properties but life itself. Some of the properties of life that you may see this ethereal being illustrate are the human being, the animal being, the insect being, the amphibian being, and the reptilian being. A being is not any particular self-existing entity as you may think. A being is an existence illuminating itself as a presence, and even though the physical eye cannot see it in its entirety, the physical eye experiences a glimpse of this existence every time the human eye is able to look into those he is animating. For example, if you were to look directly into the eyes of an animal that is alive and an animal that is not, you would be able to see an acute difference in their eyes. You can clearly see the spirit of life in the animal that is alive but not in the other one. This also works when you are trying to identify someone. You may perhaps mistake them for being someone else until you are able to look into their eyes and see their actual presence. That part of you that is able to detect this apparent difference is the ethereal presence and actual core of your very existence. It is life observing itself through a different perspective and in a different form of expression. But all in all, it is the same being or presence that is the animation of it all. All the properties of life you believe are not alive, such as the mountains, trees, and the ground, are all alive and living. I would now like you to follow the train of thought I am about to express very carefully. If you take a look at the human body, it is very easy to see what parts are active and what parts are not. The eyes, hands, feet, arms, and legs are all a part of the human anatomy and play a very animated role in its operation, so much so that the determination of life is based upon the animation of these features. Now the ears play a very important role in the existence of the human being, but do not appear to be animate enough. However, the ears are as much alive as the rest of its counterparts because the blood of life circulates through them as well. Now, let us compare this example to that of Earth. Imagine for a moment that the mountains and the ground were like the ears and the nose of a human body. They show no real animation or apparent evidence that they are alive, but we witness their existence everyday. Imagine, if you will, the blood of the human body being indicative to the ethereal being of Mother Earth. The blood circulates through every part of the human body, giving it life. Well, the being, or the life of Earth, does the same to all properties that make up Earth's existence, therefore the ground, trees, and mountains all possess within them the same life force that the human body has, and that is the ethereal being.

Now this being, or life, flows through every part and layer of Earth's existence. Everyone and everything is the same in one, and one and the same. There truly is no such thing as individuality in the grand scheme of how things operate. Now, I do realize that the common mind will find this information slightly difficult to digest.

But may I submit to you a different perspective on things? The very idea of life is a difficult one to digest when you really think about it. The human being had no desire to exist here and did not have anything to do with being born into this world. And yet, here you are, talking, walking, and living an existence you know little about. The only thing you know for a fact about this existence is that you are going to die one day. Everything else that you believe you know about was told to you either by a scientist, doctor, preacher, a parent, or a teacher. That information was never discovered by you but was given to you by those who were here before you. The majority of that information was based on assumption or a belief. So, when you really think about it, you don't really know anything at all, and with this being the case, you should be able to find it fairly easy to entertain a process of comprehension that you are not accustomed to.

Life is considered a miracle because the question of how it came to be has never been answered. Therefore life is considered to be an enigma and a phenomenon at the same time. Even though humanity has not yet been able to discover the answer to the miracle of life, you can rest assured that there is one. One of the cardinal reasons why humanity has been able to abandon the quest of acquiring answers as to why we are here, is because the liberal faculties that would aid us in the understanding of this concept has been disabled. The human being has discovered within himself a sense of worth and superiority. Therefore, control and power has become his priority so that this idea that he has of himself can be protected and respected. So, in order to succeed at this, he must first make sure that the other human beings like him never discover who and what they truly are. The organic nature of what the human being is must be compromised and destroyed so that he can be rebuilt to be a carbon expression of what he originally was. Intelligence, then, becomes artificial intelligence, so now instead of the human being using his organic ability to reason, he is depending on someone or something else to reason for him, thus creating for himself a God or a ruler. Now in order for us to be able to discover the mysteries of life, we must be able to do it using the organic ingredients that make up who we truly are. Artificial intelligence cannot comprehend an emotion or a feeling, nor can it comprehend thought and the process of critical thinking. The reason is because those attributes have nothing to do with the physical existence of the human body, but are spiritual attributes pertaining to something that is invisible and intangible. So, in order to unfold life's mysteries, we have to do it in our original state of mind and organic state of existence. The place that a thought comes from is the same place that you as a living being come from. You see, a thought is an idea or a suggestion, and once that suggestion is entertained it becomes a part of your reality. The actuality of a thought is in your deciding to manifest its intentions into the material world. So what is incomprehensible becomes comprehensible by your decision to bring it into this realm of existence. The ethereal being works in this same fashion; we are nothing more than a thought made tangible. For example, your parents may have decided in their minds that they wanted to have children before you were born, so one day they came together and nine months later you were born. The thought preludes the action before it becomes actual and visible for all to witness.

The human being is nothing more than a thought made tangible. So now the question becomes: what is the life that lives within the human, and what is its makeup? We know there is a life that causes the human to exist because the heart is beating on its own and is not plugged into anything to make that transpire. How can this phenomenon be explained? Allow me to propose the following perspective. We can all agree that the brain is the control center of the body. It is the place where all the commands of the body and its functionality comes from. And even though medical doctors know this, they have yet to entertain the idea as to where the brain is receiving its commands from. For the arms and legs to move, the brain has to give the command to do so. But where is the brain getting its commands from? Here is another perspective: your heart is beating on its own but is not being told to do so. Your body is not plugged into anything, and yet the physical body appears to be able to function independently with no assistance. Now these two perspectives are very important because everything else that shows animation and growth depends on something else. For a television to work it has to be plugged into an electrical outlet, the same with a hair dryer or a microwave. Anything we see in life that has any kind of energy flowing through it is being inspired by some outside influence, and this principle applies to an apple tree and its connection to Earth. So if we can observe this apparent feature throughout all of life's properties, then we should be able to employ in our thinking the process of trying to discover the human being's connection for its energy source.

Now to discover the energy outlet that is attached to the physical body, we have to begin at its inception. When a baby is created within the womb, its entire life dependence is based upon the energy source of the mother. The energy output for the baby is transmitted through a cord that connects the two bodies together. The baby's heartbeat, life sustainment, and well-being are supplied with energy by the mother. Once the baby is born, that energy source is broken and the baby has to attach himself to a different source of energy. When the baby enters the world, it has come into a new realm of existence and has become one with the spirit of the earth. This is the new energy source that the baby has become attached to. The beating of the human heart is in perfect synchronicity with Earth's frequency and vibration. The attachment to Earth is connected by the spirit that enters the vessel once it has arrived here. We know this is true because when the baby enters this world, if he is unable to accept the breath of life then he will be considered a stillbirth and will be unable to live here.

The breath of life you take into your vessel is the same that you share with all other vessels within this level of existence, thereby connecting you to everyone that lives and shares this planet with you. There is no such thing as color, race, or creed. Those are all devices that human beings have created for themselves. The breath of life that the baby takes at birth is the spirit of life that infuses ethereal energy into every fabric and makeup of his being. It is life itself, taking on the form and likeness of a human presence, and once again deciding to become animate through manifestation. This is the fueling energy that charges the electrical currency that inspires life.

Your existence contains the purity of thought into one complete concept—life animating within the sphere of time and space, without apparent interruptions. In other words, you are nothing more than a thought being manifested into reality, which is the true actuality of your existence. Your physical body, however, is playing absolutely no part in this process. This is being controlled and manipulated by an ethereal presence that you, the thinking being, completes the entire whole of. This ethereal presence is a part of a greater existence and we are all simply a lower part of this existence, yet the same. It is like that of a physical body—though the physical body has many parts, it is still considered one unit or a whole. There is no separation of the arm from the leg, or the heart from the lungs; it is all considered to be one body. One of the greatest tasks of life is discovering the actual consciousness of man and the purpose of man's existence. The reason why this remains a perplexing question is because we are only conscious of one thing—the creation. Within the place we call the mind, lives the location where potential realities come into existence. The fantasies of the mind are nothing more than potential realities before they are forfeited into the material world. This is the place where the ethereal being begins the creating process. There is no such place as the past, present, or future as we know it to be. There is only the simultaneous flow of energy crashing against the walls of a material existence that we created and coined as being our reality.

Creation is simply a matter of adjustments made against a singular idea of thought of a perception that has the potential of being many perceptions and not just one. It is like water. Water can exist in three states but at the same time remain in one state. Water as liquid is water, water as ice is water, and water as steam is water. The only thing that has changed is the perception, not the actual water itself. So you see, creation works in a similar fashion. The nature of creation will always be what it is, but to appreciate creation in the most purified form we must actualize it from different perspectives. The relativity can never be compromised, however the illustration can. The ethereal being is a creation that has the ability to create. The ethereal being is like water that can manifest in different forms and is allowed to illustrate existence from any perception that is desired, therefore there is no such thing as gender, God, or the like. It is what is permitted to be, and once human beings acquire the full knowledge of what is actually real, that is when they will be in the true complete oneness of the all. The expression of life is eternal and it will never end. Everything that you see illustrated in the material world around you, are simply a demonstration of realities yet to be experienced. For example, the happiness you experience here is not true happiness, for if it were you would never become sad again. Happiness can never be sadness and sadness can never be happiness. So, the experiences here are not real but simulations of the actual experience. The ethereal presence holds the responsibility of those emotional properties of life that appear to be so real to us. For the ethereal has the true knowledge of what those emotions are and has the ability to create the simulations of those emotions within the material world. It is no different than a scientist creating a virtual reality that looks and feels like the real world but is not. So, the more knowledge you gain about your true identity and who and what you truly are, the more different realities will become available to you. Consieosophy is the study of the ethereal being and its animation within all of life's properties. The human being must apply critical thinking skills to all thought processes concerning any matters if he truly wishes to find the answers to life's greatest mysteries.

LESSON 2: ANATOMY

To truly understand the full functionality of how anything works, it is always good to know the anatomy and makeup of the thing we are involved with. This is the difference between a doctor and a patient, or a mechanic and a driver. One understands the makeup of the machinery and the other one does not, which is why one can determine the problem of the machine and the other cannot. So, when it comes to the ethereal being that makes up the true core of what we truly are, we must first understand the makeup and anatomy of what we are. Along with this, we must also authenticate and prove beyond a shadow of a doubt that this is the true core of all human existence. Because Consieosophy is in the knowing of the thing and not in the believing of it just because it sounds good or appears to make sense. To truly understand ourselves and the material world around us accurately, we have to allow our minds to see the world from a logical and transparent point of view. Belief and presumptions can play no part in this process at all.

The anatomy of the ethereal being is constructed of three liberal faculties, and these faculties make up what we all consider to be the mind. The mind, from a philosophical stand point, is the place where all creation derives from. It is the place where ego and perception coexist for the sole purpose of manifesting in the material world what we all consider to be reality. Reality and perception are one and the same thing with the only difference being one has tangibility and the other has none. One is a matter of point of view, and the other is a matter of tangibility. The ethereal being is the invisible presence that dwells within the confinement of a physical counterpart. This counterpart can be an animal, insect, amphibian, or human being. No matter what container the ethereal being occupies, it is life itself in all of these forms. The entire makeup of this "being" is the composition of three faculties as follows:

- Liberal Faculty of *Logic*.
- Liberal Faculty of *Survival*.
- Liberal Faculty of *Pleasure*.

These three faculties constitute the makeup of every living thing that animates life on this planet. From the insects to the human being, every organism that shows any kind of animation has these three faculties within it, and the description of these faculties are as follows;

- Liberal Faculty of *Logic:* ability to think and reason.
- Liberal Faculty of *Survival:* ability to sustain life.
- Liberal Faculty of *Pleasure:* The innate pursuit of happiness.

All three of these faculties are made up of three inherent components. The same way a person would view a student faculty in a high school or university is the same way these liberal faculties can be viewed as well. For example, a student faculty is made up of a principal, teachers, and staff. These liberal faculties are made in the same fashion. Let us begin first with the liberal faculty of logic and its components. The three components that make up this faculty are:

- Thought.
- Reason.
- Cognition.

Thought is the foundation of all three of these liberal faculties. The mind has to first manufacture the idea before a true deliberation upon any subject can be rendered. The question about a particular matter is invoked first, and then reason administrates the process of determining what is of sound judgment and what is not. Reason is the administrative principle within the faculty of logic. It is the part of the faculty that delivers the final verdict in the course of action that the "being" will administrate within the subject. The cause and effect value is determined first within the confinement of this faculty, before administration begins. This principle is the first component to be impaired when controlling the vessel is of utmost importance, therefore it is imperative that this component is exercised and nurtured in continuity, without any outside influences. The final component of this faculty is the component of cognition. This component is influenced by the ethereal "Law of Actuality" which states that life's transparencies is one's only cognition or reality. It is by this point that the ethereal being is living in accord with all life that is surrounding him. He is completely present and is not living within a world that he may have created within his own mind that no one else has the privilege of experiencing. If there ever is a time that this component becomes impaired, the subject may be looked upon as being a possible mental health patient. But unfortunately, the symptoms are not always easily detected. There are many people living among us that appear to be perfectly coherent but in actuality are not. They live within a world that is all their own, and from the outside you would think that their behavior is perfectly normal. For example, we may consider someone that is dishonest with people to be perfectly normal and in good mental health, we just assume that they are simply dishonest. But what we do not understand is the dysfunction in the persons reasoning that is causing them to lie for no apparent reason. For if he was living in the present and actuality of things, he would be able to see the irrationality in his ways, and the unnecessary need to be dishonest.

The next liberal factuality of the living mind is the faculty of survival, and the components are:

- Thought.
- Necessity.
- Sustenance.

Thought is the component inspired by the need to live and maintain life. It is here that ideas are constructed for the purpose of creating and cultivating opportunities, that will assist them in their quest to live and maintain their existence here on Earth. Necessity is the component that deals solely with maintaining the bare necessities of life such as food, shelter, and clothing. It is here that one would make the decision to do things that they may not want to do but find necessary to do in order to survive. Logic plays a very significant role in the thought process of this component as well because in the deliberating process, one's safety and well-being is often times considered. The moral concept to this component is most of the time never considered, simply because one may believe that moral behavior has no relevance in the process of surviving and maintaining their potential life. But what one fails to realize is that this way of thinking is very circumstantial. Sustenance would be the final component to this faculty, and it deals with one's ability to provide food and nourishment for their own body. Now in the logical course of things, the component of necessity would aid this feature in choosing food that is good for the health of the physical body. However, this is not the case in most instances because of the liberal faculty of pleasure, which we will tackle in a moment. Apart of the sustenance component is the ability to maintain a food source as frequently as possible. Your where abouts and the activities you are involved in during the day will always include some aspect of eating because of this component. It is almost as important as having oxygen. Food and eating is not just a necessity for sustenance but is also an enjoyable hobby for the vast majority of us.

Now the final liberal factuality of the living mind is the faculty of pleasure, and the components are:

- Thought.
- Perception.
- Consideration.

Your thoughts within this component conspire to provide things that will release euphoria and elation to your way of living and its existence. The enjoyment of creation is very essential to your spiritual and mental health because we create life to enjoy the fruits of its functionalities. So, when it comes to the ethereal being, the enjoyment of life is equivalent. Now the component of perception deals with what is seen and viewed through the eyes of the vessel. The physical body and its senses will experience certain aspects of joy that will always guarantee pleasure and happiness. Once the body has had these experiences, it will always be a willing participant in experiencing them again. So, perception plays the role of a judge when it comes to life and its presentments. In every aspect of your life you are being given a solicitation, and every offer that is being solicited to you is promising you some kind of joy or satisfaction. Perception is always aiding you in your decision to either accept the offer or reject it. For it is based upon your experience of what is being solicited that will determine the value of satisfaction and pleasure it will bring to you.

The final component to this faculty is consideration, and this is the part of you that performs critical assessments toward all situations and circumstances that you may encounter in life. Pleasure, particularly, is always the most considered along with its presentments. When something is being presented to you as a promise of pleasure and satisfaction, your mind automatically attempts to associate that pleasure with something that you have already experienced. So, to consider what is being presented, it has to come in the form of something you are familiar with and have a pleasurable relationship with. Because men and woman are known to be creatures of habit, what is presented most of the time will always be at some point taken into consideration.

The three liberal faculties that make up the ethereal being that is your very essence are invisible faculties that cannot be seen with the naked eye but is experienced by us on an everyday basis. To authenticate these faculties, so that they may not become just a theory to us but something that is of actual fact, we must examine ourselves to see if these faculties are of present. For it is far easier to accept this as being a matter of fact when examining nature and all of its compositions. If we were to simply take the time and pay attention to all the simplicities of life, we would be able to clearly see how well the liberal faculties play an intrinsic part within the everyday animation of life. A squirrel, for instance, demonstrates clearly the involvement of these faculties. You may see a squirrel nibbling at an acorn for nourishment one moment, and maybe in the next moment witness the squirrel running out of the way of traffic. The trees alone can witness the playing of two squirrels running between the branches and leaves that the earth creates in solace. You can also witness a little puppy seek the pleasure and joy of his master, and when he is hungry he will become persistent and frantic. If he is ever in the way of danger, he will do whatever it takes to survive and relieve himself from the grips of despair and tragedy. So, it is not difficult for us to observe that these faculties do exist with the animation of life itself.

When observing the animation of life, we are truly acknowledging that life experiences itself, apparently without any outside influences. It is life exhibiting activity upon a stage that we can all witness to the reality of experience. We know this through experience that there is indeed a mechanical working within everything, including the things we believe doesn't require any. So, to just say that "life" is experiencing itself without qualifying a conduit for it do so wouldn't make any sense. It is like saying electricity is flowing energy but not giving an accurate description as to where. So to authenticate life, let us apply critical thinking to the subject first so that we are accurate. Let us use for water as an example. Water has the ability of taking on the shape and form of whatever container you place it in. Water also has a very alchemic value to it because it is able to transpose itself when combined with outside elements. But no matter the shape or the element it relates to, it will always be water. If we were to take water and create fruit punch, the water would then be labeled as being fruit punch and not water. The anatomy of the solution didn't change, but the presentation changed based upon the combination of an outside element. We may also relate to water as being an ocean, lake, a puddle, or even rain, but in all of these forms the water is still water. Now to further authenticate water being what it is in all of these forms, we would have to recognize its features. If we were to look at an ocean or a lake we can clearly see that one is bigger than the other, but we can also observe that the substance is exactly the same. The anatomy of the ethereal being works in this same fashion; life is the ethereal being animating its existence within every property of what we all consider life.

The word ethereal is a philosophical term used to describe something that is intangible but has a very esoteric value to it. For instance, oxygen can have a very ethereal value to it because it is something that we cannot see, but we know that it exists because it gives us life. So when we use the phrase "ethereal being," we are speaking about an intangible presence that authenticates its existence by displaying itself as life animating life. Since consieosophy is knowledge through observation, then the task that we all must take in authenticating this presence, is finding commonality and patterns in all things that show life and animation. We can do this by first listing some common features that all life's animation has within it. We would also have to note that these features play no part in the physicality of the animal, human, or species because they all would differ. So, let's start this off by listing the two noticeable spiritual features that all life has in common:

- Emotion.
- Intuition.

Now the two spiritual attributes that all life shares are emotion and intuition. These are considered to be spiritual attributes because they show no display of actuality within the material world, but you know they exist because of their expressions. Emotion is a spiritual attribute that moves all living things that abide within the sphere of the earth. It is the connection that bounds all living things together with the ingredients of empathy and passion as its genetic makeup. The human being's emotion can easily be seen when there is love for a family member or loved one. This expression has nothing to do with the physical attributes of the person. It is being expressed because of a connection that they have toward that person or individual. An animal's emotion can clearly be seen in this same fashion—the protection of his master or offspring is because of this same connection. Intuition is your innate impulsion of knowing that something is occurring or is about to occur. It is able to feel what is in the future and what is in the present simultaneously. That is why animals can pick up the feeling of a presence and can sense when there is danger around. The human being has this same ability but because of the psychological distortion, this perception isn't as keen.

It is an undeniable fact that all life exists transparently without the aid or help of the human being, therefore eliminating the idea of the human being playing the God complex within this realm of life. Life is expressed by animate and inanimate properties. Every animate property of life has one common denominator and that is the eye. All living creatures that move about freely on this earth have eyes that witness everything. The inanimate properties of life—such as the trees, plants, land, sea, and water—do not have eyes. But we do know that they are all alive because they show an apparent generation and degeneration property, for things that are not alive do not express these features. Now the animate properties of life—the humans, the animal kingdom and all other species—have the one thing in common, and that is the eyes. The eyes of each one of these living creatures are used to observe the world by perception and to be a witness to all creation. Each creature lives and dwells within its own habitable environment. Now the eyes have a very unique quality to them because they only represent a window or lens that can be looked through to view a display of some sort.

Somewhat like that of a telescope or a pair of binoculars. So with this being the case, the question would then become: who or what is actually doing the viewing through each particular lens? There has to be someone doing the viewing because the eyes are only the makeup of the machinery but not the actual operators. If we examine the human being and the anatomy of how he is made and constructed, we can clearly see the differences between the eyes of each vessel. You see the eye represents mystery because the actual viewer cannot be seen with the naked eye but can be expressed through his various actions. We know that the eye is a mystery because when you're meeting people for the first time there is no sense of familiarity; there is only curiosity. Therefore, the viewer is a mystery to you until he has revealed himself through his manifestations.

Until this has happened, you will never truly know who and what you are dealing with.

The eye is the witness to information in all of its forms, and in every animate property of life we can clearly see that they all have this feature. The viewer that is viewing the world through the windows that we call the "eye" do not know who they are. But what we do know for sure is that it is a presence or a being that we are interacting with. This life force is experiencing itself on every level of consciousness, including the lower one that we are experiencing now. It is the "you" and it is the "I" that lives within the confines of a physical body. Now the character you were designed to play on the ethereal stage of life is only an exploitation of a design that you were predestined to play within the realm of existence. What you have to realize is that consciousness does not mean that you're alive; it only means that you are conscious. You know this to be true because when you were born into this world, you had a life before you were conscious of the fact that you were alive. Because you cannot recollect the events that transpired during the early stages of your time here does not mean that you were not here. So, in the same fashion that this could be a reality, could it also be possible that you had an existence before this one but you are just not allowed to recall it? I assure you it is very possible. There are ethereal laws that govern life and all of its properties, and these laws are spoken about extensively in my prior work "Man, His True Essence." The distance between this world and the astral world in degrees is so far apart that your level of comprehension is too minuscule to comprehend.

Your mind is only allowed to be married to the world that you have been placed within. To gain true enlightenment about any other world, you would have to leave this one first. Your adventures within this state of existence are merely replications of things that have already been played out. You are truly the mockery of a reality that has already transpired, but because of the distortion within the core of your existence that you have allowed to happen, you are unable to see reality as it truly is.

The anatomy of the ethereal being is the actual core of what you truly are. You were not designed to be controlled or manipulated, to be subservient to something that is less greater than what you are. However, if you allow your mind to be interrupted with devises that are of your counter, which have only intentions of harm toward you, then your mind will be forever dilapidated because of the nonsense. Humanity is so used to the tangible that we are unable to appreciate the intangible things that is truly life itself. Humanity has been programmed to follow traditions and to have faith in what has been passed down, without the permission of asking questions that may secure true understanding of himself and what his true make up really is. If you were to pay close attention to the most basic elements of life, you would find the answers to the most complex questions about it as well.

LESSON 3: INTELLIGENCE

One of the most important attributes of any life on this planet is the intelligence module that lives within the center our creation. Intelligence is a conglomeration of knowledge that one has absorbed about himself and the world around him that becomes the very oracle of information that he uses to navigate himself throughout the world. It is knowledge personified into the very mind of the actual individual for what you know becomes your God, which is why it is most important that one acquires the right amount of knowledge. Information and knowledge are two entirely separate things. Knowledge is acquired through one's own personal experiences, and information is something that is given to you as proposed knowledge. Information is a property that belongs to the family of artificial intelligence; it is not acquired through experience, it is simply given to someone or something. If you have ever used a computer, it is very easy to see how this process works. A computer operates on certain programs such as Microsoft Office or even Adobe flash player. These programs are simply devices of information that once injected into a computer delivers certain amenities to the user. The desktop itself does not possess any knowledge of its own; it is simply a conduit used to administrate information that it has been given. Knowledge is a property that belongs to intelligence because it is a property belonging to its own environment. Therefore, it can only be acquired through experience and the relationship that one would have with the world. Now the unique quality of intelligence is that it is without prejudice and is with sound acuteness and authenticity when it comes to comprehending the world and all of its properties. Because the knowledge acquired through experience is so personal, it essentially becomes a part of the very being of the vessel itself, therefore making it impossible for anyone to take what has been known to him.

One of the differences between knowledge and information is that one is learned and the other is psychologically absorbed. Artificial intelligence learns information, and intelligence absorbs knowledge. We can use a computer again as an example. Because learning is a process, computers are designed and constructed to be able to accept information that is being given to it. Once a program or software is downloaded, the computer has to process the information before the user can began to use the program. The computer has to learn the information before it can properly administrate your permission to use it. You see, learning is a process that takes time and patience. Whenever something has to be learned, it is usually because someone has given you information that you have to become familiar with as it is foreign to your organic way of thinking. It is not something that you have personally experienced; it was something that someone has given to you so that you can adapt to its way of functionality. This way of thinking is completely unnatural to actual intelligence itself, and this is why so many of us have such a difficult time learning new things. Learning is a process that belongs to the artificialities of life and things. Intelligence does not have to learn anything because within its very structure lives a psychological sponge that acquires knowledge based upon experience and not assumption, and because knowledge is acquired in this way the intellect becomes a part of the very being of the individual or vessel.

Knowledge is the foundation of intelligence. The earth that we live in has an ethereal intelligence that is unprecedented. We witness this intelligence everyday of our lives, from the shifting of the seasons to the movement of the oceans. There is, indeed, a divine structure to everything that exists within the confinement of this earth. For example, if you take a look at every creature that exists in our world, there is a divine intelligence keeping order. The birds were given wings because their purpose is flying; all other creatures that do not possess wings cannot fly. Even the human and his design was very well thought out, with legs being the main part for mobility, and arms used for aid in transporting the vessel. The hands and fingers are used for grabbing and holding things. This ethereal intelligence of the earth cannot be denied, nor can it be held in speculation, but if we are disconnected from Earth and all of its inhabitants that share this space, we will become artificial. The knowledge then has to be learned and not acquired because our level of comprehension will not be able to perceive things that are real without the prospect of it being a conspiracy or only theory.

Now the reason why the world is being viewed in the way it is being viewed by the majority of the human beings that live on this planet, is because humanity has been disconnected from its life source, which is Earth, and has been reconnected to a program. When we are given facts about Earth and the ethereal nature of its existence, we are mentally trained to believe that this way of thinking is a conspiracy or a theory that has no real substantial facts supporting it. Because your mind can only relate to things that it has been exposed to or has had some kind of relationship with. Take a cloud for instance. The human would look at and discover shapes of things that he recognizes here on Earth that are tangible. But in all reality, the cloud does not possess any shape at all; it is just a cloud with no form of its own. But because we can only identify inscrutability with things that are comprehensible to us, our minds began to create similarities so that we can mentally digest what has been seen or discovered. This works in the same way with everything in life that the artificial mind is being introduced to. It is just like the search engine Google. If you type a request for information in the search box, the search engine will return to you everything that relates to what you are searching for. An artificial mind works in this same fashion; it can only relate to things that it has been familiarized with. So, in order to understand your true makeup and the world around you, you have to first reconnect to the very life source of your existence, and that is Earth. Your mind has been trained to place importance on things that really holds no real importance or value—things like entertainment celebrities, social media outlets, favorite television shows and the like. But the things of this life that hold true value and substance, we give very little to no importance to them. We show no reverence for the sun that supports the very life on this planet. Humanity would prefer to praise and adore an entertainment celebrity before giving any praise to the sun for supporting their very life. So, you can see clearly how artificial intelligence lacks reason and true substance, which is the very reason why the world is in this condition today. The world has now come to a place that requires the human being to return to his organic way of thinking and intellect. We must now awaken the thinking mind and leave the artificial world to return to the ethereal world, for this is the natural habitat of the living being. The reason why this is of most importance is because we are now living in the age of ACI or the age of Artificial Computer Intelligence and programming. Your places of employment are now converting the use of human involvement to artificial technology, which means that the need for physical workers will soon be eliminated. Your way of living has now been reduced significantly to that of a computer screen so much that human contact has become null and void. Communication has now become cyber and internet based, so the emotional value of the human has now been lost and replaced. If the human being is not able to awaken the thinking mind, the only solution for him will be annihilation; for artificial intelligence cannot coexist with someone that is similar. It would be like a cartoon character trying to survive in the real world—the actual human being would have the advantage because reality would be his native state of existence, whereas the cartoon character would not because his habitation is artificial.

Now let us talk more about the ethereal intelligence, and I am truly hoping that you are following my train of thought so far. The ethereal intellect that Earth possesses was inherited by the Earth's parent, who is in the center of all ontological life and existence. This presence is intelligence itself and is a very intricate part of the fabric of life and all properties associated with it. This very intelligence that is responsible for the placement of objects orbiting in time and space lives within every aspect of life. This intelligence is the reason why the day and night have their perspective order, and why the sun is the perfect distance from Earth. Without ethereal intelligence there would be no day and night, no moon or sun, or life on this planet or others. Because the earth is connected to the ethereal and we are connected to the earth, this makes us ethereal as well. This means that the same ethereal intelligence that is responsible for the sun being a certain distance from

Earth, the seasons changing, and the rotation of day and night, is the same ethereal intelligence that lives within humanity and every living creature that walks the face of this planet. This also means that with this ethereal intelligence must also live an ethereal being. Since this intelligence is so supreme and ethereal, it also has the ability to create intelligence itself, and because it is something that is being created and is not an intrinsic part, it can only be artificial. So, if the ethereal being has the ability to create artificial intelligence for other ethereal beings the question would then become why? And what would be the purpose? The interesting thing about all of this is that ethereal intelligence has the potential to manipulate others of the same kind into a lost perception or identity. This will be elaborated more in my next work of science fiction, The Identity Crises. Unfortunately, I am sad to announce that this is exactly what has taken place within the very core of humanity.

As I stated before in an earlier chapter, consieosophy is knowledge through observation, understanding life through experience. With this being the case, one would have to observe the manifestation of ethereal intelligence to truly know for a surety that it exists. The reason why I am raising this point at this time is because "deity" or "God" is normally who one would regard as being responsible for the aforementioned actions, but I would submit to you this: can one truly authenticate a deity that has never been seen or experienced and hold him responsible for all that we can see and experience? Could it be possible that a creation can be seen and the actual deity or God that created it can never be seen? My critical thinking in this matter only suggests this to be a plausible argument because the populous that would respond to such a question are the very ones that have experienced a creation and have had the pleasure and honor of meeting the creator face-to-face. Therefore, logic would, at some point, have to ensue and become the common ground. Now intelligence is intangible but can be observed and experienced through manifestation. I would not need to connect intelligence to anything because it is a part of everything that lives and exists. We can all agree that we have had the honor of experiencing intelligence. For everything that lives has intelligence living within.

You see, the reason why it is difficult for us to comprehend things that are not of common nature is because we have all been programmed to see and view life a certain way. A child, for instance, does not view the world the same way an adult would, because a child has no limitations and has not been told that there are such. Therefore, the child is free to feel and experience life organically without interruptions, hence why he is able to walk, crawl, and breathe on his own without anyone teaching him how to do these things. What we must do as human beings is understand that we will never truly be able to comprehend what life is all about. Your comprehension is only relegated to a range of perception that you are not allowed to go beyond. Now there are some who have exercised their faculties in such a way that they have seen the astral world and life beyond what we have experienced and are able to witness things that I am speaking about in this work. But for those who have not, this knowledge can be truly difficult to digest and accept as being true, for truth is experience and everything else is a lie. To understand ethereal intelligence, one has to first know and understand themselves because that is where the answer to your existence lives.

What is perceived does not constitute actuality, and we witness this as a fact on an everyday basis. The evening news will always create a perception that is totally different from the way circumstances actually are, and the reason why things are this way with us is because this is how things are in the grand scheme of things. For example, the sun appears to be closer to Earth than it actually is, but because of our perception and how insignificant we are, it appears to be a lot closer.

The sun appears to be rising and setting everyday but scientists say that effect is due to Earth's rotation. Now using my intellect, I can clearly see that Earth is perceived to be performing actions that it is not actually performing, which would then persuade me to question creation in this same matter. Could it be possible that we are a creation that presumes our creator to exist in the likeness of what our minds are accustomed to? Would a creature that is made of a likeness presume his maker to be of the same? Could it be possible that creation as we know it to be has a creator who is not in the same form? I would presume that the very dynamic of life and all its properties consist of contrasting features. For there are creations that live so far beneath the earth that mankind has been unable to discover them. I would have to conclude that perception is the variable to all of humanities conclusions for we can only relate to what our minds can perceive. And if this is true, then the answers to life's most difficult questions about existence can never be truly answered here. Here is more food for thought—the very idea of a man has a very interesting artistic element to it. He is made of flawless, detailed parts that have a purpose. The conception of this idea holds a very valuable question: what was the conception before man's design was solidified in creation? In other terms, man itself is only an idea. We cannot be so naive to believe that there have not been other kinds of creations. It is like the creation of an automobile and the creation of a house. Both of these creations exist simultaneously but are not of the same blueprint and anatomy. One has mobility and the other does not, one has wheels and the other has stairs. So just consider for a moment a creation of an animate life existing at some point totally different from the life you are familiar with. I assure you, it is very difficult for your mind to fully grasp this concept because our perception is too limited. It is like being at a baseball game and not being able to make out the players. Until you are able to get a closer view, your perception of what you are viewing will change.

So you see, trying to understand life from this point of view can only be accomplished by having ethereal intelligence to comprehend an ethereal creation. We can all recognize the proceeds of this intelligence through the works of such inventors like Nikola Tesla, Thomas Edison, and Henry Ford. These inventors did not have to attend a university to create their inventions; it was solely based upon their ethereal intelligence through their connection to the earth that allowed these inventions to become manifested within the material world. In a similar manner, obtaining knowledge through observation and understanding the world through experience would aid you in the survival of yourself and your mind. Artificial intelligence must be alleviated from your existence entirely. You must awaken the thinking mind to become aware of the illusion that you have so injuriously been placed under.

LESSON 4: CONSIOUSNESS

To become aware of an existence outside the control of your own volition is considered to be a miracle in itself. We are born into a world that has a preset reality for us to accept without any previous consultation about it. We are made to believe and follow the positions of humanity that have been prepared for us and will be ridiculed if we choose not to support the status quo. So, what we subsequently become is a sea of followers that will go along with any doctrinal jargon and affiliation that makes sense to us. And by doing so, we believe that the things we follow and experience are things we are consciously subscribing to. To fully understand how the psychological submission process works, we would have to first understand the aerial divisions of our makeup that would allow us to adhere to such rhetoric and intellectual complications.

The human being, along with all other life on this planet, is able to comprehend the world through a metaphysical sensory called consciousness. This is the part of you that is aware of an existence and can navigate through life based upon the familiarities you have been accustomed to. It is the part of you that allows you to appreciate all the major and minor properties of this existence. Now the word consciousness has two meanings associated with its expression—the word consciousness which means "awareness" and the word conscience which means "with knowledge." Both meanings are relative with the only difference being one is a product of "actuality" and the other has knowledge of that actuality. The world today has both of these terms misconstrued because of various popular nuances and social rhetoric. Because we are in the age of knowledge, the world has accepted spiritualist doctrine such as the "law of attraction" and spiritualism as its main ingredient for the acceptance of someone being awake or asleep. Without humanity ever getting the full story, they have run away with this ideology and have created a segregated society based on a teaching they know little to nothing about.

The doctrine I am relaying to is speaking about consciousness as if it is something that makes one superior over someone else. If someone is conscious, this philosophy is being taught to mean that they are spiritual. But if someone is conscious or aware of something, it would be impossible for this to insinuate that the individual is some kind of special creature, because to be conscious of something only means that you are aware of it. For example, if I am conscious of a wall in front of me, this just means that I am aware that there is a wall in front of me, and I can now move in a particular manner because of it. This does not mean that I am special in any way. Now if someone has conscience, and has knowledge about a particular subject, this does not make the individual special. For a man can acquire knowledge but if he does not acquire wisdom he will just become a foolish man with knowledge. What humanity fails to understand is that just because you are conscious does not mean that you are alive. You can acquire all the knowledge in the world and be aware of the most esoteric mysteries of the world and can still be considered a dead man walking. You see, life is not about consciousness, it is about comprehension and perspective. All our lives we have been given a perspective that has secured a particular level of comprehension that limits us in our ability to truly engage in the true essence of life itself, and because of this we are experiencing the world upside down instead of right side up. Death, for example, is considered as something that ceases to exist, but death is very much the contrary. Death is actually the true beginning of life in its truest illustration and completeness. It is the transposing of one thing leaving a state of existence to simply enter a better and more appealing one. It is like a caterpillar shedding its formal state of expression to undertake a greater and far more appeasing one. So, one may ask if this is truly what death is, then what is life?

Life is death and death is life. What you perceive consciously as being life is really death. To further prove this point, please provide your interest within this train of thought—from the day you were born you were being prepared for death. As you grow through the various stages of development, you reach a point of degeneration when your body begins to change and you become older and weaker as you age further. So really what you are experiencing is death but in a slow process. You are literally experiencing death on a daily basis because every single day you are losing cells and you are losing energy, so the life that you believe that you have, you truly do not. Life is prosperity and goodness in its purest form, and the very essence of life is prosperity and nothing less. If something is not prospering that means it is becoming deceased and it is not producing energy, which means that it is not alive. Life can never die because it goes against its very nature; for its purpose for existing is prosperity. So, if you find that you are slowly becoming deceased then you are not really alive, you are only experiencing a mock illustration of life. What you must understand is that those who believe they are conscious are actually are not. Nothing is really what it appears to be. Things are only suggested and prescribed to you based upon your obedience to its regimen. For example, the majority of the spiritual community believes that every human being has a subconscious. But if you review nature and the natural order of how things work, you can clearly observe that nature does not provide a substitute for anything. The tree does not have a substitute for its roots, and nor does the bird have a substitute for its wings. So why would the human being, who is made of the same properties, be designed any differently? What one has to understand is the divine design of their makeup. There is no substitute for consciousness; there is only consciousness and unconsciousness. The part of yourself that you contribute to the various phenomena you may experience within your vessel, is the part of you that is actually conscious. The subconscious part of you is the tangible attributes of your existence that you experience from day-to-day. And because you are not living in the real world and in the true actuality of things, life perishes quickly and withers away because it is not real; it is only an illustration of reality but is not reality itself. This is the reason why this state of existence is known to be the subconscious. For real life never dies or ceases to exist. It is infinitely sewn within the fabric of immortality, therefore making it impossible for you to be conscious of it because it does not exist. To truly be alive is to live in a reality that has no restrictions and no boundaries, for it has never been your physical body that has been alive, it has always been your mind. The mind never dies, and neither does the knowledge that you have within it.

AWARENESS

Your knowledge of actuality is the part of you that is having this experience we call life. So you can be conscious and at the same time be dead, and you can also be alive and at the same time be unconscious. The organic essence of life is prosperity and in order for things to prosper, there are certain elements that need to be present. The ingredients and anatomy of life causes prosperity in the inception process and cultivation of living things. Such ingredients would include love, benevolence, trust, selflessness, charity, devotion, reciprocity, strength, and wisdom. These ingredients are the corporation of life itself, for it is without prejudice and does not see life in parts but as a whole. So, for one to say that they are alive because they are conscious would be inaccurate if they are not within the ethereal makeup of the aforementioned attributes. One must truly allow himself to view the world from all perspectives and not just from a singular one and he must allow himself to be conscious of all aspects of the world and himself. Because to truly be conscious is to be consciousness itself and to not just be the possessor. One has to embody the entire concept to be truly effective, and by saying that you are conscious you are only insinuating that you are in the possession of something that is outside of your own material makeup. What this means is that you have not truly awakened at all because awareness is being aware of itself and all other properties that exist, for awareness is the all-encompassing of life. And if life is awareness then it is impossible for life to ever violate itself. Someone who is truly conscious would not hurt people or injure them by disturbing their peace of mind. They would not disrespect the earth by spitting on it and would not harm animals or any other living creature that walks the face of the earth. Because they are consciousness itself, and their awareness is panoramic and all-encompassing, they are able to feel the intimate vibration of life's animation with all living creatures that share the same space and time.

Now for one to have knowledge or to be conscience is a very good beginning point but it is most advantageous to become knowledge itself. You are a walking body of knowledge within the very structure of your physical body. Your hands, feet, legs, arms, and body—all have knowledge that is being communicated daily with the world. So, the physical body that you inhabit is actually knowledge itself, walking and living. The part of you that is aware of the physical counterpart is the part of you that is the design of ethereal knowledge. This is why mentors and professors are always telling us that we all have greatness within us, we just have to activate it; and that is exactly what has to be done. Because the core of your existence is ethereal, you are not able to learn things and acquire information, you are only able to remember. Knowledge has always been hidden within you, it is only a matter of remembering where you put it. Therefore, you are not learning information; you are manufacturing it. Knowledge is the creator of information and because you are knowledge itself, the task is easy to accomplish. Now your mind is a place and not a thing where all knowledge dwells. Creations are created here and fantasies are proposed to be realities, but only if the "being" subscribes to it. Your conscience is only allowed to play the role of God in respect to your coherence to yourself and the world around you for a very short period of time. So, it is of most important that you recollect who you are in the becoming of knowledge and all of its informants. Once you find the ethereal knowledge that is within, you will realize that God has never been that far away from you. True consciousness is consciousness within the ubiquitous transitions of awareness.

God is simply an idea and not something that is real or actual. We know this to be the case because the authentication of such a being is yet to be done. No matter the religious concept or opinion, no one has ever truly been able to substantiate the existence of God. But because there is a creation in existence, we automatically presumed that there has to be a creator, or a God of some sort, responsible for it all. The God concept is an ideology that derives from Greek mythology and is a deity that requires your faith and belief in him to exist. Because it is mythological, it is not based upon any factual evidence but is solely authenticated through stories and fables that intertwine fiction with reality.

The important element of God or deity is his ability to deliver and secure one's human infirmities and shortcomings. With this being the case, it is very easy for humanity to subscribe to this idea because humanity itself bears many human infirmities. As I stated previously, your mind is a place where fantasy is transposed into potential realities, so one would have to ask oneself, is the human mind conscious of God? And what is meant by conscious awareness? For us to answer such a question, we would first have to establish what constitutes awareness or consciousness. Awareness is a perception of reality that the mind chooses to inhabit the entire embodiment of. It is based upon the conglomeration of one's experiences, ideas, and relationships with tangible properties that are considered to be carrying a unique sense of actuality. So, in essence, one can be aware of something that someone else isn't aware of. If this is the case, then the reality that one's mind can conjure could potentially be a fantasy made into a reality that no one else has the privilege of being a part of. This could also mean that one could appear to be living in the same reality that you are living in, but could be actually living somewhere totally different. This is the current situation that human consciousness is in. Whatever the mind can conceive, it can manufacture. Is humanity conscious of God? I would have to conclude that yes, humanity very much is, because awareness and the ideas that have been presented have constituted that such a deity actually exists. This condition, coupled with the need to serve something greater than oneself, helps convert what is only fiction to practical thought and reality to the injurious way of thinking.

Let us now unveil the derivation of consciousness, its origin, and the substantiation of consciousness itself. Everything has an origin, no matter the material value of the thing. It comes from something. Within the origin of things lives the genetic makeup of what it actually is. For example; the human body is composed of minerals and substance. Everything that is of the earth is within the composition of the human being, therefore making Earth its mother. If we were to go further we could say that Earth has an origin as well and its origin is the great parent of the human being. The human and the being that occupies the body had an origin as well, just like Earth and the human. So, with this being the case, one would have to ask what real consciousness is and what could possibly be its place of origin. Because it is something intangible, it would seem that this question would be deemed impossible to answer. But if you were to view consciousness from a unique perspective, this concept may become much easier to digest. Imagine for a moment that consciousness is water. Water is able to take on the shape and form of whatever environment it encounters, much like consciousness. Whatever environment you are exposed to you will take on a new awareness of that space and time because consciousness is adaptable. Once water is evaporated, it is able to return to a state of invisibility, so now what was once visible to the common eye has returned to its native state of existence. When water returns to this state, there are no boundaries that it cannot cross. And since there will be nothing for it to particularly take on the shape and form of, it will take on the shape and form of everything. Consciousness works in the same fashion. Your consciousness is unique because it takes on the shape and form of *your* ethereal essence. In this state, consciousness is bounded to the one mind that it has been assigned to, and just like water it can be shared subjectively in many forms and many vessels. Now once consciousness is released through the transitional process of death, it is now returning to its original state of existence which is comprehensibility, and just like water during its transition would not become a part of all forms, shapes, and vessels due to its availability, the consciousness would become the same. For now, the consciousness that was once confined within the existence of one, has now become the consciousness confined to everyone. What is the highest state of existence? Perfection; to be everything and everyone, all while being nothing. This is consciousness personified and made comprehensible, for comprehensibility occurs when all is on the same accord and perspective thought patterns. When one is different from the other, they are not understood because of their different design. But when all is on the same accord within the same design, what was once incomprehensible now becomes comprehensible. This is why consciousness can only be comprehended when it is relocated into its origin. A good example of this would be the passing of a teacher or scholar; a lot of times the lessons they were trying to teach are not understood until they have passed. So, it will be in this exact same matter that consciousness will be finally comprehended.

THE APPARATUS

For one to truly understand the functionality of consciousness, we must first examine all properties associated with the subject. During the 18th century there were a lot of philosophers that were discovering and sharing knowledge, so much so that the scholars and professors called this period "The Age of Enlightenment." It was during this time that how the living psyche operated along with all its functions was discovered. As has been stated earlier, the mind is a place where potential realities are constantly being engineered and created, and one of the most basic and consistent properties of the living mind are thoughts. Thoughts are ideas, concepts, knowledge, and opinions inspired by various aspects of your consciousness. The realities that you have been exposed to and the current reality you are now living in, will determine what thoughts will become available to your consciousness. A good example would be a grade level in school—your grade level within the academic programs will determine what kind of information you will be given to study. Thinking is the product of thought, and thinking is nothing more than a private conversation one has within the confinement of his own mind. Thought becomes action when the occupant has decided to manifest it into the material world. The ideas that inspire the thoughts that enter one's mind are all dependent upon what his consciousness has been subjected to and what it has not. Your movement in life, and the desires of your heart and mind are what will lure the relative thought patterns into your mind that will, in turn, inspire your consistent movement within Earth. Environment also plays a distinctive role in your thought patterns. The environment and its habitation will create the thread of information and knowledge that will enter the mind during these periods of time. Because thoughts are not tangible, they have no restriction in how and when they will enter one's mind. Therefore, they can only be prescribed ideas that have been already prepared for you to entertain, based upon your whereabouts in life and how you correlate yourself with the world, because your thoughts are the very reason you are where you are in life, and where you will eventually end up. For it was by your subscription to the ideas that entered your mind that has caused you to live in the current realities you have faced.

Now, the mind is a place that lives within all life on this planet. It is embodied within the very make of all things that exist. For example, the mind of a tree is in her roots, the mind of the grass is its soil, and the mind of the earth would be its inhabitants. The roots of a tree bear the knowledge of all that the tree will become and is intimately involved with the process of evolution that takes place. The roots of the tree communicate this knowledge to the soul of the earth, which was a part of its very inception when it was only a seed. All the nutrients and life sustenance of the tree are communicated through its roots. The seed of the tree is where the mind of the tree begins its true inception into what it would like to eventually become. For it is within the seed that the origination of all creation begins and ends. The determination of her manifestation as an apple tree, orange tree, or the like is all happening within the mind. Now the inspiration of the seed began as a thought became tangible, and is a part of the divine creation at its finest. For every life that walks upon the earth has a seed bearing its own kind. Within the very fabric of all life, this principle is always applied because it is the entire purpose of creation. Now the animal life on this planet has a mind as well as shares in common, the same process of discovery as the rest of creation. For the mind of the animal is based upon the inherent nature of the creature and the environment. Do animals think? One would have to define thinking, and if thinking is a private conversation that is going on within the confinement of one's own mind, and as a result of that thinking they will be moved to perform an action, then I would have to say, yes. Anything that is showing animate movement and an acute generation and degeneration property within the very structure of their existence is always going through a thought process. But because of our perception, it is difficult for us to conceive such a reality. Thought inspires action, because thought comes before the action. If you don't believe me, try performing an action without thinking first; it is impossible to accomplish because it goes against the divine order of how things work. Let us entertain a different perspective for a moment. If the human being and all life on this planet moves within the earth plane based upon the inspiration of thought, then could it also be possible that all creation began in this same relative fashion? And if this is a possibility then this means that there is a consciousness that is also a part of this process as well because consciousness preludes thought. The question then becomes where and what is this consciousness and how is it perceived? At best we can all be aware that this consciousness exists but to fully understand it, we would have to alleviate to this state of consciousness.

MISCONCEPTION

One of the greatest misconceptions is knowledge without proper explanation, and in the subject of consciousness there is a lot of it. There was a film that surfaced within the conscious community titled "The Secret." This film was created for the purpose of trying to explain a spiritual law and the process on how to make the law work for you. Now because societies are motivated by greed and selfishness, the law is a part of a process that is supposed to attract to you the things that you want and help you to detach from things you do not. In the film, the universe is mentioned and how it is always working in your favor. Let us first analyze what a universe is. The word universe has two separate meanings—the word "uni" which means "all in one" in Latin and the word "verse" which means "to turn or translate" in Latin. So the true definition of the word is "all translates in the one accord."In other words, everything that exist makes up the collective whole. So when one says that the universe is doing something for them, what exactly are they referring to? Is it the solar system that scientists say make up the entire world? Is it the planets and the galaxy that we and Earth are a part of? One would have to truly qualify such a statement, because without qualifying it becomes an ambiguous suggestion, furthermore leaving one with the idea that the thing they are speaking about is a person or a God. Now let's just assume that the universe is what is being referred to as God. You would now find yourself in more of a quandary about the matter than you did before. Because then you would be assuming that deity is the collective universe, and ultimately, the creator of all things, which does not make any logical sense at all. The world operates on dependency and it is an erroneous thought process for one to believe that this is a plausible argument. If you truly think about how we communicate with each other on a daily basis, you would clearly see how much we depend on each other. For example, a mother depends on her place of work to support herself and her family, and the children depend on their mother to support them. The same goes with the place of employment. The employer depends on the efforts of their employees to move the company, and the employer depends on their customers to support them. So, if you really examined the collective whole from a conglomerate point of view, it would appear that everyone is playing God in some respect. For if God is the giver of life and the protector of it, then I can presume only through observation that we are all playing an intrinsic part in this role. The mother would be like God in her children's eyes because she is the one providing and protecting them. The workplace would be God in the mother's eyes because it is the one providing income and financial protection that the mother needs to take care of her children.

The cardinal point that I want to get across is that theoretical principle is only there to direct you to the actual principle, for it is not the theory that provides the solution; it is the truth behind the theory that does. The misconception that is alive within the minds of the conscious communities is that there is some outside force helping you navigate through life, when it is actually the other way around. *You* are the actual force, not a universe or God, and we can provide many examples that would qualify this statement. What the human mind must understand is that the body he inhabits is only a tool, and he (the occupant) is the actual user of the tool. The tool has no animation of its own until the user decides to animate it. The universe that many speak about is indicative of a classical orchestra. All of life's properties—visible or invisible, animate or inanimate—makeup this orchestra. Not only are the things that you can see with the naked eye apart of this orchestra, but the thoughts and energies of mankind, and every living thing that walks this planet are as well. In front of every orchestra there is a conductor, and so the question should be: who's the conductor? The answer is *you*. You are the conductor, and you are indeed the orchestrator. For the universe is my orchestra and I am its conductor; for I create the sound and I moderate the various tonalities of life. This is the reality that your mind must arrive to. The universe is not doing anything, it is you doing things for it. For you are the master of the universe and not the other way around, and in all actuality it is the ethereal that you must come to because it is indeed who you truly are.

LESSON 5: ALCHEMY

Along with this concept, one must entertain the various compositions of life and all of the inherent ingredients that coincide with its animation. Because when we can understand accurately the intrinsic makeup and design of anything, it not only becomes comprehensible to us, but also becomes much easier for us to associate with. All of life's properties have been proven through science and research to all who share and possess the same compositions, which would mean that everything that is living—animate or inanimate—are all the same properties, just in a different form and manifestation. This mechanical design correlates directly with what scientists know as alchemy.

Alchemy deals with the connectivity of living things to one another, and the adoption of the idea of indivisibility in contrast to its connection to all things that exist. A good example of this concept would be that of a pound cake. The entire creation would be like a gigantic pound cake, and even though there are many ingredients involved in its creation, it is still considered to be one cake. The creation is indicative of this idea in that, all things that make up creation and its very existence share the same components and structure. Having this knowledge through the conduit of one's own personal experiences would render one the ability to adjust life's circumstances and outcomes according to his own will and purpose. For if one knows what ingredients are needed to make a cake, he may then, through the act of creative thinking, be able to use those same ingredients to make a cupcake or a pancake. The possibilities of new creations coming into existence would be endless because of the transpositions that can, at anytime, take place. Through observation, it is obvious that there is indeed a creative mechanism taking place because of the various manifestations of the same creation in different forms.

This is why the human body has to digest food in order to live. The body must constantly be replenished of any minerals and substances that are lost through the different processes. The food that the human body digests goes through three transitional periods—the first is the source, the second is the breakdown from the source, and the third is its breakdown due to the consumption process of the human body. This is alchemy in its simplest explanation, and if this concept can be understood it will be very easy to apply it in every phase of our existence.

Communicating this knowledge through propaganda and rhetoric would cause one to believe that there is some kind of esoteric connotation to its relevance, but this is sincerely not the case. This concept is nothing more than the natural order of things and how they work, and if one truly understands life and its connectivity to each and every living thing, then alchemy will be very easy for him to illustrate. All creation is a gigantic alchemic algorithm illustrated in different forms and measures. So, it is necessary that one understands that transformations and transpositions are both apart of our inherent makeup. The evidence of this being a fact is within the very examination of our own life experiences—the emotional transition from happy to sad, and economic transformation from poor to rich are both good examples of one exercising their alchemic abilities. Being aware of this ability, and having the knowledge of how this ability works, leaves one without excuse for any mediocrity in life. Because if one is successful, all is successful, but it is the realization of this knowledge that renders victory and freedom from distress. No one is better than the other; we are all made of the same ethereal material like all living things that exist. The correlation of alchemy and you will not be difficult to understand if it is observed and experienced.

REINCARNATION

Along with understanding the correlation of all living things in respect to their relationship with each other, there is another aspect to this equation that we must entertain. Within every animate property of life lives the core of its existence—the ability to replicate itself infinitely and prolifically. This ability enables the living being to leave one state of existence for the purpose of re-establishing into a new one. We can observe this feature easily within nature and its inhabitants—a lion will, at some point, impregnate a lioness, creating the possibility of him having a male seed of his likeness. An apple tree will bear apples with seeds that will allow the possibility of more of the same, while also giving proof of its immortality. So, what is happening in nature is not merely the concept of a seed providing potential for the prosperity of its own life; it is the recycling of life itself. You see, the true meaning of life is prosperity, and within the very activity of this action, continuous perfecting is going on, that is apart of an endless process beyond human comprehension. For the demise of anything is only the beginning stage of an evolutionary endeavor, designed with the purest intentions of returning to its original state of existence, which is perfection itself. We can easily observe this reality once again by taking a closer look at the activity that we all participate in the most—the act of breathing. The air that we inhale can exist within three states; solid, liquid and gas. The most perfect state of this existence is the state with the least restrictions, and the highest concentration of ubiquity; for water is everywhere and at the same time, nowhere.

Now let us examine this concept closely. H_2O as a solid has many restrictions in that it cannot promote itself within any new atmospheres unless it is given permission to do so, nor can it dilapidate itself without the appropriate influences. The solid state would be its lowest state of existence, until the influence of the environmental precipitation causes the solid to melt. Once this occurs, the solid has now been promoted to a new state of existence in the form of a liquid. Now H_2O in this state has now been made perfect through the process of evolution, for the restrictions it once had are no longer apart of its vitality. Because now, in the form of a liquid, it can take on the shape and the form of its environment, and because it is formless it has a variant sense of ambiguity and impartiality. For in a liquid state, particular elements can be allowed to invade its composition without completely destroying the integrity. Particular soft drinks such as fruit punch, soda, and lemonade are allowed to exist because the property of H_2O has allowed this to occur. So you see, just within the premise of a solid graduating to the state of a liquid, there is indeed a great perfecting quality to the entire transition. What was once a limited idea has now evolved into a perfect and sound reality.

The highest level of existence is the one with least restrictions; therefore, it is most important that the perfection of freedom always remains the objective. So, if H_2O as a liquid still bears restrictions, it is important that it evolves into a state without any restrictions at all, and this is the state of gas. For it is in this state that it can be everything and everyone yet at the same time be nothing. For in this state you cannot visibly see oxygen or air but you can feel it; you cannot taste it, but you can inhale it. It is in this state that H_2O has reached its ontological perfection, in that its final state of existence was inherently its first. It has returned to perfection but will continue the demonstration with the help of life's properties of influence. So what will then occur is the reincarnation of H_2O in the various states of existence for the express purpose of reaching its ultimate level of perfection. Examining this illustration can allow us to understand the true significance of reincarnation and entertain the possibility of our own inherent design being a relative of the same course, because throughout life we are always looking to do better and be better at doing. This inherent desire could very well be apart of a much deeper and meaningful truth that we have not discovered yet. For it is by careful observation, and our experience with life, that we can justly conclude that without progression we would be a lost generation, retarded in our own designs and efforts. With this announced, we would have to take a closer look at the very nature of our existence and the irony of it all, without prejudice.

The human being that lives on Earth is the most enslaved and confused of all living beings. He is born to a state of servitude, with freedom given to him based upon a design that is not of his own cognizance. Though he does not owe a duty of care to anyone, he is made to believe that he does and will live the majority of his life serving everyone but himself. It is apparent to us that such reality does exist but we have not yet taken the time to truly understand why. To be born into a world of slavery and then to live seventy-five years in this state only to die, seems not only ridiculous but also pointless. What could truly be the point of it all?

To answer this question, let us observe ourselves and the world around us so that maybe we can find a redeemable answer. It appears to me that all the properties of life that exist showcase an apparent reason for existing in some fashion or another. There also appears to be a certain quality of rhythm and harmony between all properties of life that are animate and inanimate. There is a particular divine structure that is in place, keeping order and tranquility. We can see this within the animal kingdom, the amphibian plane, and the like. The birds have wings so that they can fly and appear to live a very structured lifestyle without change. There also appears to be certain divine laws in place, keeping them from interfering in the affairs of life that is not of concern to their own. The fish that swim in the sea do not appear to have a desire to abrogate the liberties of the animals that walk upon the earth, and the animals do not appear to have the desire to want to abrogate the liberties of the human being. However, when it comes to the human being, there appears to be an obvious disconnection between nature and himself. The human appears to want to conquer and control every property that constitutes life and its components. The abrogation of liberties is not the only desire he carries toward nature and the animate life that it inhabits, but he wishes to abrogate the liberties of his own kind as well. The homes of the forest animals are destroyed because the human wishes to pursue his own ventures and designs. So, it appears that the only component of life's design that is without order and structure would be the human being, which would then inspire two very interesting questions: What steps need to be taken to make the correction and what caused this disconnection in the first place? To address the first question, we would have to first examine the nature of mankind and his reasons for superiority.

Now there is no such thing as "disease" in nature, but there is, however, a "disease" in man. This disease exists because there is a divine purpose, rhyme, and reason for it all. Mankind appears to be more intelligent and wiser than nature and its inhabitants when the opposite is the case. For nature is innocent and only carries the desires for peace, harmony, and prosperity. Now if we apply the example that was used earlier about H_2O and its liberation to perfection, we should be able to see a small glimpse of truth in this analogy or at the least a seed for thought. Let's imagine for a moment that humanity is H_2O living in its lowest possible state of existence—that of a solid. In this state, he has many restrictions and has been reduced down into a state of consciousness that carries so many limitations that he almost does not exist in the grand scheme of things. However, the nature and pedigree of his design is well intact, even though it is not noticed apparently. He carries a God complex because within the fabric of his very design he is life itself in its highest point of existence but has been reduced to its lowest. Because life is about the continuation of constantly perfecting what is imperfect and producing the very prosperity that we all exist in, then the life within the "ethereal being" would have to continue on the same course. So then, what we would have set up for mankind is an obstacle course, a game, and a test. And each time this test is taken, the human being should be getting closer to his origin and native level of perfection. Each time the test is failed he must repeat the course until the test is passed and the obstacles have been overcome. Perfection is love and love is perfection, and to truly exist, one must exist as love itself, without separation. The obstacles within the course of the human's artificial life will be everything opposed to the nature of love, and the game that he will be forced to play will challenge the nature of love; in that it will be filled with activities that can only inspire the opposite.

The test will be his obedience to the convenient that was placed within the soul of his existence, that he knows he should obey but is tried every day in ways that he shouldn't. This is reincarnation; the truth behind the skepticism, the lie, and the rhetoric. Mankind fears what they do not know, therefore knowledge is freedom from fear. To be fearless means to be all knowing and always obeying the ethereal laws that constitute the very fabric of your being. You are in essence "real life" playing a part in your artificial life, which is only a fiction, an artificial reality created by you and for you. We will all see paradise but very few of us will see heaven; the hell that men speak about is an internal condemnation that renders a suffering that involves the demoting of a state of existence that can only be inhabited by those that are of the same kind. It is very indicative to the fable spoken about in the holy book of revelations; "There was a war in heaven. Michael and his angles fought against the dragon and the dragon was casted down." It is a story about the "ethereal being" warring with himself meteorically with the connation of esoteric knowledge imbedded within the text. There is no such thing as hate, there is only love and the constant prosperity of life in all of its final designs.

ESOTERIC NUMEROLOGY

The answer to life's most difficult questions lives within the truth of our very existence. We, as human beings, automatically create things that are in the image and likeness of the things that we experience. Within the normal course of our creative endeavors, we measure the possibility of new creations by using science, rulers, and guides that have been proven to be effective in past creations. And while doing this, we never stop to question how science, rulers, and guides came into being and all of the divine reasons as to why. To truly comprehend these processes, we must understand the divine order that life and all its properties follow without failure. Sacred numerology is the science of how numbers work, the definition of numbers, what they represent, and the correlation of those numbers to life and how they correspond to the connectivity of our designs and ambitions. To understand sacred numerology, you have to first understand what each number means and represents, for every system used in our world today is being guided and designed by using some form of numerical system. There is a purpose behind the numerical system—for each number carries its own individual identity that helps shape the molecular structure of not only the material world, but also plays an intrinsic part in the shaping of our thoughts.

Every living species that walks the face of Earth has an inherent duality always present within. For every property of life bears the male and female counterparts, and there are certain characteristics that make up the creation of these particular roles. For example, we know that the male counterpart is always the most dominant and does not need anything or anyone to exist, he just exists. The male is the giver of life and designer of all prosperities that derive from his presentments. The female counterpart is the one that aids in the preparation of life and plays the role of the receiver and nurturer. Now, the reason for these two counterparts coming together is for the purpose of prosperity and the continuation of life's designs. The purpose of the female coming together with the male counterpart is to prosper and bring forth some kind of fruit that will yield evolution and prosperity within Earth's plane. This is the whole purpose and design of the female—to assist the male in efforts of prosperity. Once the female and male have made their connectivity, they can begin to bring forth life and fruition; before this happens no life or fruition can be made possible.

Let us begin to express the correlation of numbers and their relativity to life and its properties. Now the first number of the divine numerical system is the number zero, and this number represents the abstraction in the ambiguous role of numerical value. Because it does not hold a particular value, it plays the role in the summation of all numbers within this system, and the illustration of its design explains very eloquently its purpose, which is to always exist. All the other numbers within the system can be added or subtracted but when it comes to the number zero, there is no adding or subtracting because it is infinite. To further emphasize its design, the multiplication of itself will be expressed by the selecting of the mirror of continuity that will show one "0" on top of the other, illustrating the continuity of life without distraction. This will then mutate into a number that will have a numerical value, which later became the number "8." The second number of this divine numerical system would be the number "1." This number represents singularity in its very design; for it is self-sufficient and holds no desire to be otherwise. The collaboration with his design is always welcome, but the integrity of his independence will never be compromised. Now because there is no aid needed to exalt the value of what this number is, he represents the male gender because it will be via multiplication that all the other numbers will be allowed to come into existence. For without him, no other number will be allowed to exist independently because he will be the main ingredient needed for their existence.

The next number within the divine numerical system would be the number "2." The number "2" represents the female, for she is the born application of a male reproducing himself within the world of duality and contrast. Because it is the "1" reflecting him from a different perspective, like that of a mirror holding the same image but from a different point of reference.

Because the number "2" in and of itself cannot hold any value without the aid of the number "1" playing an intrinsic part, she will always be the lesser and the subjected. Now a good example of this union would be a father and mother to a daughter. The daughter is nothing more than the genetic creation of the parents coming together as one to bring forth life. And within the very core of her existence, she is nothing more than the expression of father and mother as one single life, as a reflection of the two.

Now the next number within the divine numerical system would be the number "3." The number "3" represents the male within its design because its dominance represents structure and foundation. For example, the equation for all living species within the earth is considered to be

Father + Mother + Offspring = Family

This is the divine structure of any creation, incorporeal or corporeal, for even the material structure of any building has within its make up the discipline of the "3" key elements—the blueprint, the materials, and the workers. The number "3" represents government and is illustrated by the geometric shape of a triangle. Even within governments you have an executive branch, legislature branch, and a judicial branch. This is the structure that holds order and administration. So, whenever the symbol that you see below is expressed or illustrated, you are witnessing some form of government structure. It does not mean evil or anything that you may consider strange or outside of the normal context of discussion. It is simply government and structure.

The next number within the divine numerical system is the number "4." The number "4" is nothing more than the prosperity element that lives within the very nature and core of life's design. For it is the multiplication of the number into a greater state and form of herself, it is like a little girl growing up to become a beautiful woman, but it is only a stage and is not a final destination for her growth. Within the very illustration of her design, you can clearly see the feminine attribute that she bears and the maturity that she has from the growth of her previous state. For now she is more structured in her physical design whereas before there was less structure.

The next number within the divine numerical system would be the number "5." The number "5" represents the male gender, and just like the number "4" is only the maturing of a previous state before, the number "5" shares the same fate in rendition. He is government improved and perfected, and this is why the physical body shares in this perfection the various illustrations. For the hands are joined with five fingers and the feet joined together with five toes. Now in some animals, you will see the feet and hands joined together with three extensions, which is giving the same concept of government.

The next number is the number "6." The number 6 represents female and she is nothing more than the growth from her previous state. Within her design is the prosperity of physical life accompanied by the promise of pleasure and lust (I will explain more momentarily). Now the next number within the divine numerical system would be the number "7" and he represents the male gender, and of course he is the progression of his previous state, in that he has been able to elaborate to further perfections within all of life's designs. For example, there are 7 days of the week to denote the completion of a cycle. It is the perfection of the five days that man works and the resting of the two days for replenishment. Now the next number within the divine numerical system would be the number "8" and she represents the feminine gender. Within her very design, eternity is defined because she is never-ending and never beginning. We can also see this illustrated in the shape of a woman because her material body is shaped in the form of the number "8." This is a direct expression of life and the vehicle that will be used to express its final designs. For life is everlasting and can never die. The final number within the divine numerical system would be the number "9" and he represents the male gender. He is the completion and final level of growth within the course of his existence. He has now reached a level that can only grant him access to the inheritance of the final level, which is complete perfection.

Before we go on to show the numerical system and its prosperity, we will make this a more personal and intimate endeavor by expressing how these numbers are indicative to human cognizance and life. We will first begin our discourse with the woman; a woman goes through four stages of development before fully becoming a woman and these stages are:

1. Baby Girl
2. Little Girl
3. Teenage Girl
4. Woman

Each one of these stages is represented with a numerical value and they are as follows:

1. Baby Girl =2
2. Little Girl =4
3. Teenage Girl =6
4. Woman =8

The number "2" is the baby girl because it is her first inception into the world and experience with life and all its properties. The number "4" is indicative to the little girl because this is the stage of structure and growth; because she is now becoming aware of her existence and is becoming more familiar with life's structures. The number "6" is indicative of the teenage girl because this is the stage of sexuality for the young women, and is usually the time when she is beginning to experiment with intimacy in all of its brands. The number "8" would be indicative to woman because this is the stage of completion in the identity of what she truly is. It will be at this stage that the experiences of life will begin to shape her perception of herself and the world that surrounds her. Her desire to prepare life becomes a part of her final destination within life's designs. Now the man also goes through four distinct stages of development and they are as follows:

1. Baby Boy

2. Little Boy

3. Teenage Boy

4. Man

Each one of these stages is represented with a numerical value and they are as follows:

1. Baby Boy = 1

2. Little Boy = 3

3. Teenage Boy = 5

4. Man = 7

Now the reason why the number 1 is indicative to a baby boy because he is self-contained and has all the potencies of life and the prosperity of it living within his very being. Because the seeds of life will allow him to give more abundantly in time, so long as there is a soil available for him to plant the seeds. The number "3" is indicative to the little boy because this is the stage of structure. During this time in the young man's life he is given instruction on how to interact with humanity and the rules that apply to societies' moral concepts of right and wrong. The number "5" is indicative to the teenage boy because in this stage he has established within himself a sense of self. He has grown into his own personality and has begun the process in determining where he should end up. The number "7" is indicative to man because this is the full structure and final design of his existence.

Now to ensure that potential energies are at their ultimate perspective, it would take the greatest effect within the nature of life's transpositions and collective correlations. The only way this can be done is through the uniting of each numerical value for an absolute effect. And just as a child will one day leave his father and mother to become one with his wife, so must the numerical system perform the same. So now, you will have the repeating of the same in numerical order but joined together with a counter. The beginning of this sequence starts with the number "10" which, of course, represents immortality. For this representation expresses the number "1" being the beginning and ending, but with the company of the number "0" enforcing its immortality. Now if we were to move along this sequence, we can see how life is reflected within the numerical value of numbers. For example, the number "11" would represent two men, the number "12" represents a man and a woman, and the number "13" represents two men again. Now as I stated earlier, life is all about prosperity and whenever there is a lack of prosperity you will find disorder and dysfunction. This is one of the reason why the number "13" is considered to be an unlucky number, for there can not be prosperity or life from the union of two men. No fruit can possibly come from this union, therefore the fruit that it will try to bare will be spoiled and tarnished. The number "12" is another good example of the effect of numerical designs; for we use this number as a ruler of completion. This is why we have 12 months in a year, and why it is also referenced in Christianity as being a symbol of faith. The Jews reference the Israelites in the bible as having 12 tribes, and Jesus having 12 disciples, and of course time is measured in two groups of 12. So, we can evidently see the prosperity between the joining of these two numbers together, and all numbers within the divine numerical system will show the same or an apparent contrast.

It is most important that we become familiar with life's designs and structures because nothing is done without structure and order. There is a cause and effect to everything that transitions through life; the controlling elements that are responsible for these actions are the elements that we cannot see. We can feel them and know that they exist, but because we cannot see or handle them, we do not give complete credence to their existence. Understanding the various tools that life has given us to adequately live and adjust, will enable us to navigate life with little to no injuries to ourselves.

AWAKENING THE THINKING MIND
Consieosophy is the ability for one to acquire knowledge through observation and the

ability for one to understand life through experience. But in order for this to be a possibility, one would first have to detach themselves from their formal way of thinking to reattach themselves to the organic way of thinking that was a part of them before the programming began. Humanity in the 21st century suffers from a lack of knowledge and spiritual dehydration, so much so that it has lost the ability to think and is now under the spell of an artificially designed system that controls their every thought, impulse, and activity. If humanity does not awaken their ethereal senses, they will be exterminated and done away with. We must allow ourselves the right to reconsider the world that we live in and the right to analyze its properties and its orders. For this is not a generation of leaders but of followers, this not a generation of knower's but of believers. So without any contest, we can conclude that without change, this generation will create a future less prosperous. It is most important that humanity awakens to the truth of who they really are and what constitutes them being who they are. We can no longer afford to be distracted by the mediocrities of life anymore and the pleasures that are habitually being handed to us on a daily basis. We must begin to activate our minds and begin to view life from a spiritual and ethereal point of view instead of a carnal one. For we are not carnal creatures, so it would only make sense that our attention should be placed on the things that are most essential to our existence, and those things are not tangible.

To truly understand and comprehend the ethereal being that animates life through every property that constitutes life, we must first open our minds and eradicate any parts of our being that desires to create conflict against various perspectives, rather true or untrue. For when we are in discussion about any particular matter, we are not having the conversation for the sake of proving a right or wrong perspective, but it is for the purpose of coming together to agree on one perspective or truth. Critical thinking is always the ruler of conversation and humility, and an open mind will foster truth and harmony within the sphere of the discussion. So, no matter what the discussion is about, we must always express truth about what has been observed and what has been experienced on our behalf. By doing this, we enable ourselves to challenge spurious truths, doctrinal dogma, and religious tonalities for the purpose of understanding what is actually experienced and known as being a matter of fact, and what is simply a matter of opinion.

The objective of this work is for all to not only come together on one accord in various life's matters, but to also become a leader and ruler of one's own principal dominion, which is their physical body. Consieosophy is indeed the future of humanity and the answer to all societies. Governments will no longer be needed because the people will be able to successfully govern themselves. There will be no need for law enforcements because the laws will already be in the people to govern them, and there will be no need for money because humanity will be the exchange for goods and services. This work is for the seeker that endeavors to find the answers to life, himself, and the world that surrounds him. For the answer to the worlds' troubles are in the understanding of life and all the properties that are associated with it, because it is knowledge through observation, and understanding life through our experiences that will ultimately free us from fear and ourselves.

QUOTABLE QUOTES

1. Humanity is so used to the tangible that we are unable to appreciate the intangible things that is truly life itself.

2. If you pay close attention to the most basic elements of life, you would find the answers to the most complex questions about it as well.

3. Truth is experience and everything else is a lie.

4. To understand ethereal intelligence, one has to first know and understand who and what they are.

5. A man who acquires knowledge but does not acquire wisdom will only become a foolish man with knowledge.

6. Knowledge has always been hidden within you; it is only a matter of remembering where you put it. Therefore, you are not learning information, you are manufacturing it.

7. True consciousness is consciousness within the ubiquitous transitions of awareness.

8. A man will live many lives within his lifetime, so he must make certain to never

recall characters from his other lives into his present one.

9. I am so contrary to popular belief that you would question your beliefs in conversation with me.

10. The personality is a personification of one's own character and attributes in a more palatable form.

11. I do not want to learn anything but I wish to absorb everything.

12. Man must adopt the abilities of becoming diplomatic, sagacious, and compassionate. Humility is the main ingredient for success,

for the ability to fully think before actually speaking is not only a template for the wise but is also a stumbling block for the foolish.

13. If this was real life you would never have to worry about death.

14. Move swiftly through time, sparing not even a second for wasting. For time cares for no one except himself.

15. The greatest lie ever told about life is that it ends.

16. Just because you're awake doesn't mean that you're alive.

17. Reincarnation is the continuation of life, expressing once more her need for perfection.

18. I feel that the purest of hearts, with only the purest of intentions to care and show benevolence to all living things, inanimate and animate—and to also acclaim all that is within them to good works of charity and goodwill—will graduate on to a greater existence, far beyond what the human mind could ever imagine.

19. Information is acquired; knowledge is absorbed.

20. There are no wrong answers; there are only perspectives of the right ones.

21. What is the highest state of existence? Perfection. To be everything and everyone, while at the same time being nothing.

22. Desire when fueled with determination will captivate success.

23. Your wish is the only thing that your mind can generate and bring to life at the same time.

24. The only thing that matters is what thoughts will become tangible and what thoughts will not.

25. You don't want the story to end because you have no idea how it began.

26. The universe is my orchestra and I am its conductor.

27. There is a mechanical working in everything, and this also includes the things that we believe doesn't require any.

28. My body is nothing more than an imposter casting a reflection of my true image.

29. Where there is no harmony there will be harm.

30. The Earth did not inherit me, I inherited it. Therefore, freedom is a gift, not a liberty.

31. Theoretical principle is only there to direct you to the actual principle. For it is not the theory that provides the solution; it is the truth behind the theory that does.

32. The actuality of your existence contains the purity of thought into one complete concept—life animating within the sphere of time and space without any apparent interruptions.

33. Creation is simply a matter of adjustments made against a singular idea of thought of a perception that has the potential of being many perceptions and not just one.

34. There is no such place as the past, present or future as we know it to be. There is only the simultaneous flow of energy crashing against the walls of a material existence that we created and coined as being our reality.

35. If it were possible, I would bring everyone back to life . . . if it were possible.

36. The eye represents mystery because the viewer cannot be seen with the naked eye, but can be expressed through his various actions.

37. What you have to realize is that consciousness does not mean that you're

alive, it only means that you are conscious. You know this to be true because when you were born into this world, you had a life before you were conscious of the fact that you were alive.

38. The distance in degrees between this world and the astral world is so far apart that your level of comprehension in this state of existence is too minuscule to comprehend.

39. Artificial intelligence learns information, but intelligence absorbs knowledge.

40. The interesting thing about all of this is that ethereal intelligence has the potential to manipulate others of the same kind into a

lost perception or identity. (*This will be elaborated more in my next work of science fiction, The Identity Crises*)

41. Nothing is really what it appears to be; things are only suggested and prescribed to you based upon your obedience to its regimen.

42. To truly be alive is to live in a reality that has no restrictions and no boundaries, for it has never been your physical body that has been alive, it has always been your mind. The mind never dies, and neither does the knowledge that you have within it.

43. It is by careful observation, and our experience with life, that we can justly conclude that without progression we would be a lost

generation, retarded in our own designs and efforts.

44. Perfection is love and love is perfection. And to truly exist, one must exist as love itself without separation.

45. You are in essence "real life" playing a part in your artificial life, which is only a fiction, an artificial reality created by you and for you.

46. Forget about a spiritual awakening; awaken your mind.

47. I don't care to be understood, just comprehended.